Ten Buddhist Meditations

An Introduction To Meditation For Beginners

Tenzin Chadari

Copyright © 2023 Flow Publishing88

All Rights Reserved

flowpublishing88@gmail.com

Table of Contents

Introduction............1
Shamatha..............20
Vipassana..............24
Body Scanning.........28
Maitri..................32
Tonglen................36
Visualization..........40
Trataka................44
Mantra................48
Mala Beads............52
Shunyata..............56

Introduction

Meditation can feel a bit confusing if you're just starting out. It's unclear if you are meant to shut your thoughts off through pure force of will, or are we meant to ignore them? There seems to be some mysterious goal at the end called enlightenment but that seems so abstract and disconnected from our daily lives.

Besides, it has to be difficult or boring because you are sitting still for so long. There are plenty of things to do with your day that don't involve just sitting there. If you wanted to be lazy you could sit in front of the TV. At least there you have something to watch.

Despite all this meditation is quite common and growing in popularity. People want to connect with themselves and meditation has proven to be a way to do that, even if it doesn't make sense at first.

This book is meant to introduce beginner meditators to various types of meditation in the hope that they will find which style best fits what they want out of their meditation practice. It can also be a great reference for intermediate and advanced meditators as a reminder of all the options available or as a way to easily introduce others to the practice.

Meditation is not exclusively a Buddhist practice but it does play a central role in the religion. We are going to look at meditation through a Buddhist lens to help us understand the physical, mental, and spiritual benefits available to practitioners. As a first step let's ask the very basic question: What is meditation?

Meditation is a practice, similar to weight lifting, where the practitioner exercises the mind to improve attention, concentration, and emotional stability. When you go to the gym, there are different exercises you can do that strengthen specific parts of the body. The same is true specific parts of the body. The same is true in meditation.

Once you learn what the different exercises are you can use them at appropriate times to produce the desired result. In the gym, if you want to improve your bicep you can do a bicep curl. If you want to reduce stress and mental tension on your meditation cushion you can do a body scan. Don't worry. I'll explain what a body scan is later. For now just know that each exercise or type of meditation is focusing on a different aspect of the mind and by combining them we can get the results that best suit our purpose for meditating.

A basic meditation would be mindfulness meditation. Mindfulness has become a bit of a buzzword and probably means different things to different people depending on the context. When someone says they are trying to be more mindful, they might be saying that they want to have more gratitude for the good things in their life. They could also mean that they want to be more empathetic or considerate towards others.

For our purposes, mindfulness refers to a quality of your consciousness that is characterized by a feeling of openness, clarity, and focus. That might sound like a bunch of vague gibberish so let's try to get more specific.

When you are doing mindfulness meditation you are focusing your attention on the breath. Technically you could focus on anything but the breath is constant, rhythmic, and always available which makes for a convenient point of focus.

By focusing on your breath you are not attempting to control it or wrap your mental 'fingers' around it. You don't have to do anything to keep breathing, breathing just occurs. This is great because you can practice watching something that is very close to you without getting caught up in it. If you try, you can make yourself stop breathing. It's not hard. We hold our breath every time we swim. So it's a great intermediate activity. We can control it if we choose but it also happens spontaneously if we let it.

Before we get too carried away in the abstract let's return to what mindfulness meditation does. We focus on the breath. Letting it spontaneously arise. Inhaling. Exhaling. Inhaling. We live in a world of stimulation and our minds will reach out for stimulus if we have not done this very often. Our thoughts will race. Our eyes may open even though we wanted to keep them closed. Our hands might fidget.

But none of this really matters. You don't stop it from happening, instead you are learning to not let it distract you from the task at hand which is following the breath. If you practice this often enough you'll get quite good at not getting distracted. At the same time, your mind will become used to the stillness and stop producing as many distractions.

This process of improving your attention span and calming your racing mind is referred to as taming your monkey mind. There are plenty of other resources which go into this in more depth and I encourage you to read them.

I'd rather focus on what happens after this taming occurs because it helps when trying to understand why anyone would bother doing this. Once you are able to direct your focus of attention and not be pulled every which way your brain wants you to go, you begin to realize how your mind works.

Just as your breath happens spontaneously, much of your mental activity arises without much input from your conscious awareness. Before practicing meditation, because the mind drags your consciousness around, it feels as if your consciousness is producing everything but it's really not the case. Thoughts bubble up from your subconscious and float by. Emotions come to you without you deciding to feel them.

Everything that happens in the mind is quite similar in fact to how the breath works. You can exert influence over it but ultimately it is working under its own directive. This matters because we actually use up a lot of our mental energy, what I like to call our mental bandwidth, on mental activities which are going to occur regardless.

Imagine if you were under the impression that if you didn't consciously choose to breathe you would stop breathing immediately. A lot of your mental energy would be spent on breathing, leaving little room for other things like groceries or work or your vacation.

The same is true of our thoughts and emotions. They happen naturally. Spontaneously. By practicing mindfulness we are practicing opening up our mental fist which is gripping our thoughts so tightly. Don't worry, you don't stop thinking. It's a common misconception that the purpose of meditation is to rid yourself of your thoughts.

What does happen is a lot of the stress and tension we feel from this useless pursuit of identifying with our thoughts is released. We have more bandwidth to fill with our surroundings. Colors seem brighter. Sounds have more flavor. Conversations are not interrupted by tangential trains of thought. And yes, pain is more vibrant. You get both the good and the bad side of a richer texture of sensation.

It's not a silver bullet. It doesn't solve every problem you may have in your life. But it is helpful and makes challenges feel approachable, less titanic. Mindfulness is the foundation for the other types of meditation. You don't need to be at peak mindfulness to try other forms of meditation, though.

Understanding what you are trying to achieve you can better understand what it is you are spending your time doing. In the same way, by understanding that the goal of lifting weights is to increase muscle and reduce fat it makes more sense why you would want to spend time repetitively moving heavy objects around.

Meditation didn't begin with Buddhism but Siddhartha Gautama, the founder of Buddhism whom people often refer to as the Buddha, was a strong proponent of the practice. He made it a core tenet of his spiritual teachings, that meditation was the key to understanding the mind and therefore the self. When you realize the ultimate nature of your self, Buddhism teaches, you realize your own Buddha nature.

But what does that mean? Buddha translates as the Awakened One. This was a title given to the Buddha by others who perceived him as a spiritual master. Buddhism teaches that your Buddha nature is already here in the present moment with you. You do not meditate and gain something, you meditate and realize something that is already here.

Trying to explain what this something is is notoriously difficult, like describing color to a blind man. Unfortunately, no matter how much time you spend and how lovingly and painstakingly you try to describe color, he will not really realize what color is until he opens his eyes and sees for himself. No one can see color for him and give him that knowledge. It is experiential, one must experience it to know it.

But an attempt can be made to describe the way. This predicament of being unable to give someone the experience of Buddha nature is referred to symbolically as grandmother's finger pointing at the moon. The moon is the object we are discussing, the finger is me trying to discuss it, but it is up to you to stop looking at my finger and follow it to what it is pointing to. If you only learn the finger, you'll never see the moon. And the moon is the whole reason for pointing.

Buddha nature can be described as unchanging, timeless, and always present. In order to discover something so subtle you must first train your mind to be able to notice subtle things. You practice meditation as an exercise in sharpening your mind until you are capable of noticing something so subtle that it never moves and it never leaves, has always been with you and in fact exists everywhere. It doesn't happen the first day.

But honestly there are lots of reasons to meditate. Many meditators are not pursuing mystical experiences at all. The physical and mental benefits of meditation are well documented. They range from better sleep to treating depression and anxiety. Lowers stress and increases patience. Decreases blood pressure and lowers your heart rate. Who doesn't want to live a happier, healthier life?

Just five minutes a day can improve your mental and physical well-being considerably. That's a good return on investment if you ask me, with the exception of getting bored. In some ways you are channeling boredom into something useful but meditation can be fun. If you sit every day for two weeks I guarantee that by the end you'll look forward to your time on the cushion. It's a moment of self-care, a gift to yourself.

The rest of this book is an introduction to ten meditations that Buddhist practitioners use. Some are quite simple, requiring only a little of your time. In others you'll need an object of focus, like a candle. I've tried to order them in a way that marks progression, with the first meditation being the most basic and the tenth meditation being the most advanced, but it's all relative to you and your spiritual journey.

There are no requirements on what order you go in but I would highly recommend starting with Shamatha, the first meditation dealing with mindfulness. Although you could do the others first, mindfulness meditation really is the foundation of meditative practice. It allows you to foster the mental tools and experience necessary to understand what the other meditations are trying to do.

Before you can cook, you need to learn how to chop vegetables and turn on the stove. Mindfulness meditation is the practice of chopping vegetables. Shunyata meditation, the tenth meditation on emptiness, is a very nice meal that you can prepare once you understand the fundamentals.

The second meditation, Vipassana or insight meditation, could be considered the second fundamental exercise. After mindfulness becomes familiar to us, we can then begin to use it to understand ourselves. You are taking your expanded view and applying it in a practical way. Once you have these two fundamentals down, the other exercises will feel like a natural progression from where you are.

The practice of meditation has been around for a very long time. Some scholars date it back to 5,000 BCE. For 7,000 years, the human species has been sitting and watching the mind move. When you sit on your meditation cushion, remember that you are one meditator in a long, long line of meditators. It may seem silly or boring or useless at first but for millennia human beings have found value in the activity.

After so many generations of people using and adapting the practice to fit their own needs, we are handed a wide variety of flavors to choose from. There are meditations for the secular and meditations for the mystical. Meditations for increasing energy and meditations for calming down.

It's not possible to compile a full account of the types of meditative practice available in such a short space, but I hope that this book will help spark your interest and get you started off on the journey. One of the core tenets of Buddhism is called the Sangha, which refers to the community of spiritual practitioners that you are working alongside. There are meditation centers all over the world and I'm sure there is one near you. Even if there isn't, the internet has many groups dedicated to spreading the practical knowledge necessary to begin your meditation practice.

There are also many apps that have been developed in the past few years that are interested in helping promote the health benefits that come with meditation. They offer articles and other advice from meditation teachers that can help you learn the tools available to you. They also offer guided meditations where you can play a clip of someone speaking or reading aloud to you as you meditate. Especially for those who don't have the time or desire to spend hours studying about meditation, this can be a great resource to quickly absorb important information and insight into the meditative journey.

There are so many resources available today that are created by meditators who are passionate about their practice enough to want to share it with the world. It's often a joke that people who are into meditation are really, really into meditation. Maybe it's true, but it's wonderful that a mental exercise that's existed for so long is still seen to be so valuable.

A Tibetan Buddhist master named Chogyam Trungpa Rinpoche described the practice and teachings of Buddhist meditation like bread. The recipe is very old but when you use the recipe you get fresh bread every time. There is nothing stale about the recipe, it is just a recipe. It's what is inside the recipe and what the instructions produce that matters.

An unfortunate characteristic of meditation, and spiritual practice in general, is that people who spend a lot of time soaked in that culture, long enough to begin teaching it to others, have a bad habit of cloaking the whole thing in mystery and metaphor. The practice of meditation is very simple and the results meditators see from their practice are very down-to-earth. They are practical, everyday benefits that help you live your life more true to yourself, less worried about the parts of your life you can't control, and more aware of the present moment.

The reason it is so popular is because it's so easy and makes life so much more enjoyable. If there is anything that meditation teaches it's the importance of letting go. Let go of your control and you will find freedom. Let go of your worries and you will find peace of mind. Let go of your individual ego and you will find we are all connected.

How far along this path you go is up to you. There's no right or wrong way to go about it, even if there are more productive ways to meditate than others. What I mean is that if you begin meditating you are not committing yourself to attaining buddhahood. You can just sit and meditate and learn to appreciate the present moment more each time. You can dedicate your life to the practice if you want but being a casual meditator is better for your wellbeing than never meditating at all. You get to decide what it means to you.

The Buddhists have a practice called the Refuge Vow. Some say it every day but when you become a Buddhist you are supposed to take this vow as a sign of your acceptance of the Buddha's teachings, or dharma. It goes like this:

- I take refuge in the Buddha.
- I take refuge in the dharma.
- I take refuge in the sangha.

The Buddha, the dharma, and the sangha are like three shelters which help you weather the storm of samsara, or the cycle of rebirth. Meditation is a refuge. It's a refuge from the pain of the world and the confusion of life. It is a tool to grow strong in mind and body to become the best versions of ourselves we can be.

I wish you luck on your journey.

Shamatha

Mindfulness Meditation

The foundation of all Buddhist meditation is Shamatha which is sometimes translated as mindfulness. The practice of mindfulness is something we hear about a lot in the West but the idea is not always very clear.

When practicing shamatha, there are two things the meditator needs to keep in mind. The first is relaxation. You are trying to relax your mind. The troubles of the day can cause you to tense up mentally causing your thoughts to race and become disorienting. Slow yourself back down.

The second thing is awareness. You want to relax but simultaneously you want to be very aware. In this meditation, we will be using the breath. You want to be aware of the flow of your breath as you relax. This keeps you focused.

The reason we bring these two concepts together in Shamatha meditation is that we are attempting to hone our minds in the same way that you sharpen an axe. Before doing any other meditations, your mind as your tool must be sharp and strong. If your axe is dull, you will struggle to accomplish anything.

Shamatha has many benefits, including lowering anxiety, relieving depression, improving focus and attention, and improving sleep. If your mind is strong and steady you'll find that life's difficulties begin to flow off you easier. This feeling of relaxed awareness can be a part of your life every day if you practice.

Shamatha

Instructions

- Begin by sitting upright. You can sit on the floor, on a meditation cushion, or in a chair. Keep your posture straight.

- Relax into the present moment. There's no rush to begin practice. This is your time to be at peace.

- When you're ready, focus your attention at the ends of your nostrils. Feel the air come in and go out.

- Your mind will wander, especially at first. That's okay. Just gently bring your attention back to your breath. And back to your breath. And back again.

- If you are new to meditation you may have thoughts that race through your head and pull your attention towards them. You aren't trying to turn off your thoughts. Just return to the breath.

- Try to maintain good posture but if you find yourself fidgeting remind yourself that the focus is on the breath. If your posture isn't perfect, that's okay.

- You can start by doing this for ten minutes once or twice a week. You're welcome to do more but your progress may be slow if you do less than once a week.

Vipassana

Insight Meditation

Vipassana is the second core meditation in Buddhism and is particularly popular in Theravada practices. Vipassana is often translated as Insight so the practice is called Insight Meditation.

Vipassana works best when it is coupled with Shamatha, or mindfulness meditation. Mindfulness calms the mind down and improves your ability to focus. In Vipassana, we are using that focus to gain insight into how our body and mind function.

By understanding how our body and mind function we can better understand how to relate to ourselves. It's like a driver and a car. If the driver barely pays attention to the signals it's car is flashing, like the check engine light, and doesn't really know what shifting gears or turning on the windshield wipers means, then that driver is not going to be very good at driving.

The body and mind are like that car and you, as consciousness, are like the driver. It may not be a perfect analogy but it helps us understand what Insight Meditation is trying to accomplish.

The main practice of Vipassana is called noting or labelling. You are going to enter a state of mindful awareness and focus on the breath, just like in Shamatha meditation. Only this time, when anything rises up in your mind you are going to 'note' it.

So when a thought arises you are going to label it 'thought.' And let it leave. You may think, "We need more eggs." You will note the thought but not get caught up in the train of thought about eggs, groceries, cooking, and all the rest. Same with an emotion. If an emotion washes over you, like sadness, you'll note the emotion as 'emotion.'

Vipassana

Instructions

- The key is not to get wrapped up in the content of the mental phenomena. You are labelling it as thought or emotion or whatever it may be and then returning your focus to your breath.

- Start with the Shamatha meditation first and then move to this meditation as some experience with mindfulness is helpful.

- As you learn new meditations, you can alternate between them as you please. But stick to one type per sitting.

- By noting or labelling them as their basic function you are practicing equanimity or acceptance. You are also gaining insight into how the pieces of you work together.

- The key is not to get wrapped up in the content of the mental phenomena. You are labelling it as thought or emotion or whatever it may be and then returning your focus to your breath.

- Start with the Shamatha meditation first and then move to this meditation as some experience with mindfulness is helpful.

- As you learn new meditations, you can alternate between them as you please. But stick to one type per sitting.

Body Scanning

Connecting with the Body

Meditation can sometimes become all about the mind but that's not the whole picture of who we are as human beings. The body scan meditation is a great exercise for taking what you've learned in mindfulness practice and using it to reconnect with our physical selves.

This meditation is also great for releasing tension in the body. Tension in our muscles can cause stress and anxiety if it goes on for long periods of time. Many of us spend our whole day with our muscles tensed up without even realizing it.

Body scanning brings mindfulness to the body and lets us really feel how each part of us is doing. If our thighs or shoulders are clenched and we don't notice, there's not much we can do to relax them. The first step is knowing the tension is happening.

Body scanning isn't just about connecting with our senses and relaxing the body, though. It's also a great beginner's practice for mindfulness itself. By using mindfulness to feel and relax the body, we are practicing mindfulness. By practicing mindfulness it becomes easier and more automatic to bring its benefits into your daily life post-meditation.

In brief, the body scan is done by lying down on your back. You take your focus of attention and direct it at individual parts of your body starting with your left foot and moving up to your pelvis then your right foot and up. Then move up to your shoulders stopping at your hips, stomach, and heart. Do each arm starting at the hand and then the neck up to the face and finally the crown of your head. It's easy!

Body Scanning

Instructions

- Lie down on your back. You can do this in bed but if you often fall asleep you may consider moving somewhere else.

- Close your eyes and feel your breath going in and out. When you're ready, bring your awareness to your left foot.

- Notice any sensations you have there. Is your foot warm or sore? There's nothing to 'do' with these sensations, you just want to notice and feel them.

- Move your attention up your leg. Stop and feel your left calf then your left thigh and then your left hip. If you notice any tension, try to relax your muscle into a state of calm. Do the same for the right leg.

- Now focus on your pelvis, up to your stomach, heart and shoulders. What is it that these organs are trying to tell you? Notice all the sensations you can before moving on.

- Now do the arms going from the hands to your shoulder, stopping at your forearms and biceps. Do one arm at a time.

- Turn your focus to your throat. If it feels tight or clenched, try to relax it. Now your face, then ears, and finally the top of your head.

- Congratulations, you did it!

Maitri

Loving-Kindness

Because of our meditation practice, we become calmer, more capable, and more attentive. But a tool is better in hand than on the shelf and the same goes for our mind. That is to say, we have made our mind into a tool. Now what do we use it for?

Buddhists differ somewhat on the answer to that question depending on what lineage and form of Buddhism they follow. These differences aside, compassion and service to others is a common thread that connects them all.

But before we can help others we have to help ourselves. That may sound selfish but it's true. If you are unhealthy in your mind there is no good reason to behave as if you have the answer to a healthy mind. If you did, your own mind would be proof enough.

Maitri is often translated as loving-kindness and this loving-kindness is directed inward, at ourselves. We can become compassionate and forgiving towards ourselves in the same way that we are compassionate and forgiving of others.

It may seem obvious that you should treat yourself well but many people do not. They are their own worst enemy, constantly criticizing themselves and coming up with reasons for why they aren't good enough.

They must meditate harder or they aren't a good person. They must make more money or they aren't successful. They must have one million followers or they aren't lovable.

Through the practice of Maitri, we allow ourselves to be as we are. We are not indulgent of ourselves but we allow ourselves to not be perfect. We can be who we are.

Maitri

Instructions

- Sit upright on a pillow, meditation cushion, or chair. Settle into the present moment.

- Close your eyes and breathe. By now you should be familiar with following your breath. You can focus on your nose if you like or you can simply be.

- When you are ready to begin you are going to say internally or externally the following four phrases:

    - May I be happy.
    - May I be well.
    - May I be safe.
    - May I be peaceful and at ease.

- There is no need to rush through these phrases. Say them one at a time and direct them towards yourself. Really try to say them with intention.

- Stay relaxed in the moment and the awareness of your breath. Continue repeating the four phrases until your meditation is through.

- Later on, you can do a variation on this meditation where you replace yourself with others. Say "May you be happy, etc." while thinking of a loved one, someone neutral, someone you despise, and eventually all sentient beings.

Tonglen

Sending and Taking

Although the Maitri meditation can be used to develop compassion towards others, Tonglen is more specifically geared towards putting that compassion into practice.

Tonglen is often called Sending and Taking because you are sending out positivity and taking in negativity with the breath. You might be wondering, why would I want to bring negativity in? Shouldn't I be removing negativity from my life?

That's a fair point but there's one thing to keep in mind and that is that you are developing a healthy mind, and healthy minds can process difficult emotions and sensations better than unhealthy minds. So you are like a vacuum, taking in dirt and cleaning up the place.

By sending out positivity you are giving the very best of yourself to those around you. You have an infinite reservoir of happiness and tranquility if you know how to access it and by giving out that positive tranquility you find that you never run out. You can keep sending out love and compassion forever and to everyone.

Taking in negativity is not to say that you are becoming negative or frustrated or the like. You are bringing the anger, the sadness, the anxiety, or the fear of your surroundings inside you so that they cannot harm anyone. You are pulling it in and digesting it as an act of service and of love. This is compassion in action.

It should be noted that if you are not in a healthy mind state, Tonglen may not be a good exercise for you. You must be healthy and in a good state of mind to perform this service, otherwise you will just be unhappy. In that sense it's somewhat advanced.

Tonglen
Instructions

- Sit upright in your place of meditation.

- You can close your eyes if you like but it is not as important for this one. It's your choice although personally I close them.

- Begin your attention to the breath. This time you are going to be moving emotional energy with the breath. It may sound complex but just use your imagination, it is a powerful tool of the mind.

- Imagine all of the goodness in you. The love, the calmness, the happiness, everything that is good in you and your life. With the exhale, breath it out into the world. Fill the room with your positivity.

- On the inhale, imagine the suffering of the world. This can be anything you like, no need to get too focused on the small details. Breath in the pain and suffering of the world. Bring it into yourself like a vacuum brings in dirt.

- Continue this for as long as you like. Be careful that you are not straining yourself mentally in this practice. You are a filter for the world, not a box for darkness to be stored in.

- In post-meditation, use Tonglen in difficult situations. If it becomes second nature to you, you'll find that compassion for others becomes easy and obvious.

Visualization

Imagination Meditation

Meditation is often considered passive. You sit down and try not to do anything, or so the story goes. If you're looking for an active form of meditation, Visualization may be a great option.

Visualization uses your imagination to conjure up an image which you focus on. A spiritual person may describe it as manifesting the reality which you conjure in your mind. A secular person would describe it as tricking the brain.

Whatever way makes the most sense to you is fine. What matters is that it works. For example, athletes often visualize their victory beforehand to give them an edge.

In the Buddhist context, visualization is often used to help bring compassion or loving-kindness into your life. So instead of visualizing you getting a gold medal or a bigger salary, you visualize love surrounding a particular person or light shining out from within you.

There's really no limit to the ways you can use visualization. Many people will visualize their chakras, visualize a symbol or deity and chant mantras, a peaceful place where they can go mentally, or a flower 'breathing' inside of their chest. The concept is simple but the potential is infinite.

Using visualization in your meditation has many benefits including increased creativity, equanimity, self-love, compassion, reduced anxiety, and helps you accomplish your goals.

It all depends on what you choose to meditate on. For this exercise, we are going to focus on the Buddhist visualization of loving-kindness.

Visualization

Instructions

- Sit upright in your meditation place.

- Close your eyes and feel your breath going in and out. Once you are comfortable, imagine that someone who loves you is sitting in front of you.

- As you picture them sitting, smiling at you, allow the feelings of love and well-being they are emanating into yourself. Relax in that goodness. Fill yourself with their love for you.

- If you can't think of anyone, try to imagine what it would feel like to have someone love you in this way. Unconditionally wanting you to be happy, fulfilled, and healthy.

- Once you are done, imagine yourself being the source of this love and visualize someone else to whom you can send this love. It can be one person, a group of people, or whomever you like.

- Take all of the feelings of love, the desire for them to be happy, fulfilled, and successful from inside of you and imagine it beaming out from you. Visualize it beaming out from you like a bright light filling the other person up.

- Now visualize your heart opening up completely. The light of your love is now beaming out in all directions, touching everything around you unconditionally. Try to bring this feeling into your post-meditation practice.

Trataka

Candle Gazing

Sometimes called candle gazing or yogic gazing, the practice known as trataka is Sanskrit for to look or gaze. Using a candle is common, but any object will do, because it flickers and shines. If you have trouble focusing, this movement can help keep you interested which makes it easier to keep the mind stable.

The practice of trataka is first recorded in the 15th century in the Hatha Yoga Pradipika written by Svatmarama. It's a preparatory meditation intended to sharpen the mind and prepare it for more advanced meditations which require intense concentration.

Today, people use candle gazing for many of the same reasons that make mindfulness training so popular. In an age of constant distractions, training the mind to be able to focus on one thing for longer than a few seconds is helpful.

People with anxiety have what are called darting eyes, which involuntarily jump from object to object. They also typically have a faster, shallower breathing cycle.

In much the same way that slowing down our breath and inhaling deeper can cause us to relax and help relieve anxiety, slowing down our eyes and calmly settling them on one point of attention can also calm us down.

Something to think about and try as you get more comfortable with this practice is that there are two different ways of seeing. One way is open, with no point of focus, like sitting in an open field with no predators. Another way is focused, like assessing if a bush contains a lion. Although we are focused, try to remain open. It's a balancing act but you don't want to be causing stress.

Trataka

Instructions

- Sit upright in your meditation place. Put a lit candle two to three feet in front of you at roughly eye level. You can use a chair or a box, whatever works just make sure it's stable and won't fall.

- Turn the lights off or dim them so that the candle stands out.

- Relax your breath and settle into the present moment, maintaining eye contact on the flame of the candle.

- You will likely still have thoughts rising up. In the same way as Shamatha practice, just let them be and let them go. Your focus is on the candle flame.

- You may feel yourself wanting to look away. If this is your first time with the practice it may seem confusing or frustrating that you can't keep your focus. Don't get discouraged, the longer you practice the longer you can maintain your focus.

- You can do this for as long as you like but five to ten minutes is a good starting place. You can time yourself if you like but I find the alarm takes away from the calm I am trying to cultivate.

- Don't forget to blink!

Mantra

Voice and Vibration

Mantra meditation is probably something you've heard of before. It's basically meditating with your voice through chants or phrases.

One common mantra is "OM" or "AUM" which is considered to be the original sound of the universe. It's only one syllable but through repetitive vocalizing of OM while meditating you are attempting to connect with your own Buddha-nature.

A mantra that's not from Buddhism but which many in the West have heard is the Hare Krishna chant. There's really no restriction on what can be a mantra even if some are more popular than others.

You can also combine mantras with other practices like visualization. So for example you could visualize Avalokiteshvara, the Bodhisattva of Compassion, and chant the mantra Om Mani Padme Hum. The meaning of this mantra would take up too much space but it is said that it embodies the whole body of the Buddhist teachings.

Mantras can be said aloud, whispered under the breath, or recited quietly in the mind. There are mantras associated with deities, with chakras, with patterns of healing. There's no one way to use them and no one purpose.

Pick the right meditation for you and don't be afraid to try new ones to see what you like best. Shorter is better, especially for beginners. If you are reciting a 70-line mantra it may take away from the experience if you are just starting out. You can also make one up like, "I am at peace and welcome in the world."

Mantra

Instructions

- Sit upright in your meditation place. Close your eyes and relax into the present moment.

- Begin to chant your mantra. You can do this aloud, you can whisper it quietly to yourself, or you can chant it internally.

- You can pair the mantra with a visualization if you like. If you are using a mantra of healing, visualize a peaceful place or an inner light. Deity mantras can be used with visualizations of the deity, and so forth.

- Mantras are great ways to keep your mind focused. If you feel your mind drifting off, though, just return it to your mantra and continue on.

- Some mantras are intended to be said a specific number of times. Mala beads are a great way to keep track of how many recitations you've done. This will be explained in another section.

- Chant the mantra for as long as you like, ten to fifteen minutes is a good starting point.

- There's no wrong way to use mantras but if you want to take your practice to the next level you can look into theories of vibrations. Some practitioners prefer to use the back of their throats to produce a stronger vibration.

Mala Beads

Tactile Meditation

Even if you haven't heard the name, you've probably seen Mala beads before. They are also called prayer beads and are very similar in style and function to the Christian rosary. They traditionally have 108 beads, one Guru bead which is larger than the rest, and a tassle.

Mala beads are pretty versatile but generally speaking they are a meditation aid. Each bead acts as a counter. If you are using a mantra, you can recite the mantra once and count it with a bead.

If you are doing Shamatha, you can keep track of how many breaths you've taken with Mala beads. You would inhale, exhale, and at the end of the exhale you would move up one bead.

The Guru bead acts as a start and end. You begin at the Guru bead and once you have reached the Guru bead again you know that you have done 108 breaths or recitations.

Mala beads are not specific to Buddhism but they are related to the Vedic religions such as Hinduism, Jainism, and Sikhi. Malas can be made from a wide variety of materials but gemstones, animal bones, seeds, and wood are common materials.

Each culture has its preferences and each type of material has its symbolism. For example, Bodhi tree seeds can be used to symbolize the Bodhi tree the Buddha achieved Enlightenment under. Animal bones can symbolize impermanence and the need for compassion. It's simple to make yourself or there are spiritual stores online if you want higher-quality materials.

The Mala has been around for thousands of years. Some use it as spiritual jewelry but it's also a useful tool to help you meditate.

Mala Beads

Instructions

- Make or purchase the Mala beads. Etsy is a good place to go for creative Mala creations. If you want to make your own you'll need to look for a resource that tells you what materials you'll need and how to tie the knots that keep the beads in place.

- Sit upright in your meditation place. Close your eyes and relax your mind, breathing rhythmically.

- To count with the Mala, begin by placing your thumb and middle finger around the Guru bead. With every count, move up one bead. When you reach the Guru bead again you'll have completed 108 breaths or recitations.

- If you are using the Mala beads with the breath, turn your focus of attention to the tip of your nose. Inhale slowly and exhale slowly. When you have done one inhale and one exhale you'll have completed one cycle. Move up one bead.

- If you are using the Mala beads with a mantra, start by deciding what mantra you want to use. When you have settled into your meditation place begin chanting your mantra. When you have finished one recitation, move up one bead.

- Using Mala beads eliminates the need for alarms while also keeping track of time.

Shunyata

Emptiness Meditation

Shunyata is a difficult concept to explain. It is often translated as nothingness or emptiness but this alone does not really do justice to the concept. One way of describing shunyata is the basic ground of existence. It is existence itself before characteristics have been laid over it.

Meditating on emptiness can seem frightening to some people. Emptiness is often associated with death which can be scary. But emptiness as shunyata is actually the opposite, it is life itself. It is the foundation for life.

Just as the empty space in a house lets you live in it or the empty space in a vase lets you fill it with water, emptiness as the foundation for our existence allows for the conditions to arise which let us exist. Without emptiness, there is no fullness.

But shunyata is not easily grasped conceptually, one must experience it to really appreciate its meaning. As the great Buddhist master Nagarjuna said, "To whomever emptiness is possible, all things are possible."

Meditation on emptiness works best with a teacher because there are many ways that the mind can misunderstand its meaning. If you were to only focus on this one aspect of the dharma, it would be easy to think the Buddha was teaching nihilism but he wasn't.

There is also something called the poison of shunyata. Even if you understand shunyata perfectly well, if you focus too much on it, it becomes unhelpful. One must liberate from even the antidote, as it is said, meaning that you should not use shunyata to escape life but instead to embrace life more fully.

Shunyata

Instructions

- Sit upright in your meditation place. Close your eyes and begin to focus on your breath, slowing it down to a rhythm.

- Although there are many ways to realize shunyata, we will be using a mantra to help us. The mantra goes like this: "Emptiness is form. Form is emptiness."

- The purpose of realizing emptiness is to get a better understanding of ourselves, our universe, and our minds. Try to maintain a posture of unattached awareness. Shunyata is not something that comes, it is already here you simply have to notice it.

- Because it has no characteristics, is always present, and does not change it can be very difficult to notice it. That is why we practice mindfulness and awareness so that we are able to discover very subtle phenomena.

- Chant the mantra slowly and let its meaning wash over you. It won't make sense at first and that's okay. As you recite the mantra you will intuit its meaning and eventually, through diligent practice, you will discover for yourself what the fuss is all about.

- This is an advanced meditation and I would not recommend it for beginners. I add it here as a taste of what your practice can become.